Breakfast & Brunch Recipes

Copyright 2006, Gooseberry Patch
First Printing, October, 2006

A glassful of fresh-squeezed orange juice is always a treat
at breakfast. Set out a juicer along with a bowl of oranges cut
in half so guests can take a turn at squeezing their own.

Country Breakfast Skillet

Makes 4 to 6 servings

5 c. frozen shredded
   hashbrowns, thawed
salt, pepper and garlic powder
   to taste
6 to 8 eggs
1/3 c. milk
1 to 2 tomatoes, chopped

4 to 6 green onions,
   thinly sliced
1/4 lb. thinly sliced deli ham,
   diced
1-1/2 c. shredded Cheddar
   cheese

Cook hashbrowns in a skillet according to package directions,
seasoning with salt, pepper and garlic powder; set aside. Beat eggs
with milk; stir in tomatoes, onions and ham. Stir egg mixture into
hashbrowns over medium heat; stir quickly to scramble. As eggs
begin to set, add cheese. Continue to stir until eggs are cooked and set.

Make bacon curls to garnish your breakfast plate. Fry bacon until browned but not crisp, immediately roll up slices and fasten each with a toothpick. Drain on paper towels.

Yummy Apple-Walnut Muffins *Makes 2 dozen*

2 c. all-purpose flour
1 c. sugar
2 t. baking powder
2 t. baking soda
2 t. cinnamon
1 t. nutmeg

2 eggs
1/2 c. oil
5 c. apples, cored, peeled and
    coarsely chopped
1 c. chopped walnuts
1/2 c. raisins

Mix together dry ingredients in a medium bowl and set aside. In a separate bowl, whisk eggs and oil. Fold in apples, walnuts and raisins; add to flour mixture and stir until moistened. Fill greased muffin cups 2/3 full; bake at 350 degrees for 20 minutes.

All happiness depends on a leisurely breakfast.

-John Gunther

Sausage & Red Pepper Strata *Makes 4 to 6 servings*

1/2 lb. ground pork sausage	4 eggs
1/2 t. dried oregano	1 c. evaporated milk
1/4 t. red pepper flakes	1 t. Dijon mustard
4 slices French bread, cubed	1/4 t. pepper
1/2 red pepper, diced	1/2 c. shredded sharp
1 t. dried parsley	Cheddar cheese

Brown sausage in a skillet with oregano and red pepper flakes; drain and set aside. Arrange bread cubes in the bottom of a greased 8"x8" baking pan. Top with sausage mixture, red pepper and parsley; set aside. Whisk together eggs, milk, mustard and pepper; pour evenly over sausage mixture. Cover tightly and refrigerate overnight. Bake, covered, at 350 degrees for 55 minutes. Uncover; sprinkle with cheese and bake for an additional 5 minutes, until cheese is melted.

Tuck cheery blossoms inside lots of 1950's-era egg cups and scatter on the breakfast table. They'll make everyone feel perky even before the juice is served!

Warm Spiced Fruit

Makes 10 to 12 servings

20-oz. can pineapple chunks,
    drained and juice reserved
8-oz. can pineapple chunks,
    drained and juice reserved
29-oz. can sliced peaches,
    drained
29-oz. can pear halves, drained
    and quartered

3/4 c. brown sugar, packed
1/4 c. butter
2 4-inch cinnamon sticks
1/2 t. ground ginger

Combine fruit in an ungreased 3-1/2 quart casserole dish; set aside.
Blend together reserved pineapple juice and remaining ingredients in
a saucepan; bring to a boil. Reduce heat and simmer for 5 minutes;
discard cinnamon sticks. Pour over fruit and bake, uncovered, at
350 degrees for 30 minutes, or until heated through.

Vintage-style salt shakers quickly become the prettiest little containers for dusting powdered sugar or cinnamon on breakfast treats.

Blueberry Pillows

8-oz. pkg. cream cheese,
    softened
16 slices Italian bread
1/2 c. blueberries

2 eggs
1/2 c. milk
1 t. vanilla extract
Optional: powdered sugar

Spread cream cheese evenly on 8 bread slices; arrange berries evenly over cream cheese. Top with remaining slices, pressing gently to seal; set aside. Whisk eggs, milk and vanilla together and brush over bread slices. Cook over medium heat on a lightly greased hot griddle until golden. Flip and cook other side until golden. If desired, sprinkle with powdered sugar before serving.

Invite your neighbors over for breakfast or brunch. Welcome
them with steaming mugs of cider or coffee and frosty glasses
of juice or milk. Serve favorite foods buffet-style...what a fun
way to enjoy each other's company!

Heat & Hold Scrambled Eggs

Makes 6 servings

1 doz. eggs
1-1/3 c. milk
1 t. salt
1/8 t. pepper

2 T. all-purpose flour
1 T. chopped pimento
1 T. fresh parsley, chopped
1/4 c. butter

Combine all ingredients except butter in a large bowl; whisk until smooth and set aside. Melt butter in a skillet over low heat; pour egg mixture into skillet. Cook to desired consistency, stirring occasionally. Can be held for up to one hour in a chafing dish or electric skillet set at 200 degrees.

Add some pretty lighting to your table. Tuck votives into tart pans, inside graters or on top of pudding molds or bobbins.

Sausage Rolls

Makes 16 rolls

2 8-oz. tubes refrigerated
   crescent rolls
1 lb. ground pork sausage,
   browned and drained

1/2 c. shredded Cheddar cheese

Separate each tube of rolls into 8 rectangles; press diagonal seams together with a fork. Sprinkle sausage and cheese evenly over rolls. Roll up dough jelly-roll style; slice rolls in half and place seam-side down on an ungreased baking sheet. Bake at 375 degrees for 15 to 20 minutes. Serve warm.

Keep juices icy cold for breakfast...it's easy! Fill old-fashioned milk bottles with orange, apple or grapefruit juice, then set them inside a galvanized bucket filled with crushed ice.

Grandpa's Fried Potatoes

Makes 6 to 8 servings

3 to 4 lbs. potatoes, peeled
16-oz. pkg. bacon, chopped
1 onion, chopped

seasoned salt and salad
  seasoning to taste

Cover potatoes with water in a large saucepan over medium heat; boil until tender. Drain; let cool slightly and dice. In a large skillet over medium heat, cook bacon and onion until bacon is crisp. Partially drain drippings; add potatoes and seasonings to skillet. Continue cooking until potatoes are golden, stirring occasionally.

Make someone feel extra special...serve them breakfast in bed!
Fill a tray with breakfast goodies, the morning paper and a bright
blossom tucked into a vase.

Cinnamon Fried Apples

Makes 4 servings

1/3 c. butter
1/2 to 3/4 c. sugar
1 T. plus 1 t. cornstarch
1/2 t. cinnamon

1-1/2 c. water
4 tart apples, cored, peeled
    and quartered

Melt butter in a skillet over medium heat. Stir in sugar, cornstarch and cinnamon; mix well. Stir in water and apples; cover and cook over medium heat for 12 to 15 minutes, until apples are tender and sauce is thickened. Spoon sauce over apples to serve.

Plump raisins by covering them with boiling water and allowing
them to stand for 15 minutes. Drain and pat dry with a paper
towel before adding to a recipe.

Old-Fashioned Porridge

Makes 4 to 6 servings

3 c. water
1-1/2 t. salt
2 c. long-cooking oats,
    uncooked
2 eggs, beaten
1 c. milk
1/4 c. molasses
1/3 c. maple syrup

1/4 c. brown sugar, packed
3/4 t. nutmeg
1/2 t. cinnamon
1/2 t. ground ginger
3/4 c. raisins
1/4 c. chopped walnuts
Garnish: half-and-half

Heat water and salt in a saucepan until boiling. Add oats and cook for 5 minutes; cool. Combine remaining ingredients except half-and-half in a large bowl; add to oats. Pour into a greased 13"x9" baking pan. Bake, uncovered, at 350 degrees for 2 hours. Serve topped with half-and-half as desired.

Make juice glasses sparkle! Dip the rims in water and roll in coarse sugar before filling with juice.

Mushroom Crust Quiche

Makes 6 to 8 servings

5 T. butter, divided
8-oz. pkg. mushrooms, chopped
1/2 c. saltine crackers, crushed
1/4 c. green onion, chopped
8-oz. pkg. shredded Monterey
    Jack cheese

8-oz. container small-curd
    cottage cheese
4 eggs
1/4 t. pepper
1/4 t. paprika

In a large skillet over medium heat, melt 3 tablespoons butter. Add mushrooms; cook for 6 minutes, until soft. Stir in cracker crumbs; press mixture evenly in bottom and up sides of a well-greased 9" pie plate to form a crust. Cook onion in remaining butter for 5 minutes, until soft. Spread over crust; sprinkle with cheese and set aside. In a blender, combine cottage cheese, eggs and pepper; cover and blend until smooth. Pour into crust; sprinkle with paprika. Bake at 350 degrees for 25 to 35 minutes, until a knife tip inserted near center tests clean. Let stand 15 minutes; cut into wedges.

Weekend sleepyheads love to wake up to the aroma of breakfast in the air. So, before they come downstairs, make the table look extra-special...daisies tucked in glass milk bottles and a colorful tablecloth made from vintage-style oilcloth really add fun.

Quiche-Me-Quick

Makes 10 to 12 servings

1/2 c. butter
1/2 c. all-purpose flour
6 eggs, beaten
1 c. milk
1 t. baking powder
1 t. salt
1 t. sugar

3-oz. pkg. cream cheese,
    softened
16-oz. container small-curd
    cottage cheese
16-oz. pkg. Monterey Jack
    cheese, diced

Melt butter in a saucepan over medium heat; add flour. Cook and stir
until smooth; add remaining ingredients. Stir until well blended;
pour into a greased 13"x9" baking pan. Bake at 350 degrees for
45 minutes. Cut into squares.

Vintage-style glass milk bottles add a touch of nostalgia to your breakfast table! Fill the bottles with a variety of juices or milk and everyone can choose their favorite.

Georgia Cheese Grits

Makes 12 servings

6 c. water
1-1/2 c. quick-cooking grits,
    uncooked
3/4 c. butter, sliced
16-oz. pkg. pasteurized process
    cheese spread, cubed

2 t. seasoned salt
1 T. Worcestershire sauce
1/2 t. hot pepper sauce
3 eggs, beaten

Bring water to a boil in a medium saucepan; stir in grits. Reduce heat to low; cover and cook for 5 to 6 minutes, stirring occasionally. Add butter, cheese, seasoned salt and sauces. Continue cooking and stirring for 5 minutes, until cheese is melted. Remove from heat; let cool slightly and fold in eggs. Pour into a lightly greased 13"x9" baking pan. Bake at 350 degrees for one hour, or until golden.

Kids love pancakes rolled around peanut butter & jelly!

Spiced Sweet Potato Pancakes *Makes 10 pancakes*

1-1/4 c. all-purpose flour
3 T. brown sugar, packed
1-1/2 t. baking powder
1/3 t. cinnamon
3/4 c. milk
1/2 c. sweet potato, peeled,
    cooked and mashed

1 egg
1 t. vanilla extract
1 t. lemon zest
Garnish: maple syrup

Mix flour, brown sugar, baking powder and cinnamon. Add milk, sweet potato, egg, vanilla and zest; stir until just moistened. Pour batter by 1/4 cupfuls onto a hot griddle lightly sprayed with non-stick vegetable spray. Cook over medium heat until bubbly on top; turn and cook until golden. Serve with maple syrup.

Keep an eye open for those great milk pitchers like Grandma
used to have...shaped like a rooster or cow, they add a spark
of fun to any breakfast table.

Ham for a Houseful

Makes 16 servings

4 to 5-lb. fully-cooked
    boneless ham
20-oz. can crushed pineapple,
    drained

1 c. brown sugar, packed
2 T. honey
1-1/2 t. dry mustard
1/2 t. ground cloves

Score surface of ham in a diamond pattern. Place ham in a roasting pan; insert meat thermometer into center of ham. Bake, covered, at 325 degrees for one hour. Meanwhile, combine remaining ingredients in a large saucepan. Cook over medium heat until sugar dissolves, stirring occasionally, about 5 minutes. Reduce heat to medium-low; cook for 10 minutes, stirring constantly, until glaze is thickened and reduced. Remove from heat; cool. Remove ham from oven and uncover; spoon glaze over ham. Bake for an additional 45 minutes to one hour, basting every 15 minutes with glaze, until thermometer reads 140 degrees. Let stand 15 minutes before slicing.

Add a splash of color to breakfast juices! Freeze strawberry slices or blueberries in ice cube trays. Toss several cubes into glasses of juice right before serving.

Southern Country Casserole   *Makes 6 to 8 servings*

2 c. water
1/2 c. quick-cooking grits,
    uncooked
3-1/2 c. shredded Cheddar
    cheese, divided
4 eggs, beaten

1 c. milk
1/2 t. salt
1/2 t. pepper
1 lb. ground pork sausage,
    browned and drained
1 T. fresh parsley, chopped

Bring water to a boil over medium-high heat in a large saucepan;
stir in grits. Return to a boil; reduce heat and simmer for 4 minutes,
stirring occasionally. Add 2 cups cheese; stir until melted. Remove
from heat and cool slightly. Add eggs, milk, salt, pepper and sausage,
mixing well. Pour into a greased 13"x9" baking pan. Bake at
350 degrees for 45 to 50 minutes. Sprinkle with remaining cheese
and parsley; return to oven until cheese melts, about 5 minutes.

Liven up plain orange juice with a splash of sparkling white grape juice or ginger ale...serve in stemmed glasses for a festive breakfast beverage.

7-Fruit Salad

Makes 8 to 10 servings

1/2 c. lime juice
1/2 c. water
1/2 c. sugar
2 peaches, pitted, peeled
   and thinly sliced
1 banana, thinly sliced
1 honeydew, seeded, peeled
   and scooped into balls

1 pt. blueberries
1 pt. strawberries, hulled
   and sliced
1 c. seedless grapes, halved
1 kiwi, peeled and chopped

Whisk together lime juice, water and sugar in a medium bowl until sugar is dissolved. Add peaches and banana; toss to coat. Combine remaining ingredients in a large bowl; stir in peach mixture. Cover and refrigerate for one hour.

Serve up special coffee with breakfast...add a dash of nutmeg, cinnamon or orange zest just before brewing. A drop of vanilla extract added at serving time is nice too.

Best Banana Muffins

1-1/2 c. all-purpose flour
1 t. baking powder
1 t. baking soda
3 bananas, mashed

3/4 c. sugar
1 egg, beaten
1/3 c. butter, melted

Mix together flour, baking powder and baking soda in a medium
bowl; set aside. Blend bananas, sugar, egg and butter in a separate
bowl. Combine with flour mixture, stirring well; fill greased muffin
cups 2/3 full. Bake at 375 degrees for 20 minutes.

Add whimsy to your breakfast table with vintage salt & pepper
shakers in fun shapes. Look for 'em at yard sales or bring your
grandmother's old shakers out of the cupboard!

Patty's Hashbrown Casserole *Makes 12 to 15 servings*

30-oz. pkg. frozen shredded
    hashbrowns, partially
    thawed
10-3/4 oz. can cream of
    mushroom soup

8-oz. pkg. shredded
    Cheddar cheese
2 T. butter, melted

Mix ingredients together in a large bowl; spread in a lightly greased
13"x9" baking pan. Bake at 350 degrees for 30 to 40 minutes.

Company coming for brunch? Take it easy...the night before,
mix up dry ingredients for muffins or waffles, chop veggies
for omelets or whisk eggs for scrambling. The next day,
you'll be a happy hostess.

Asparagus & Tomato Quiche   *Makes 6 to 8 servings*

1/2 c. onion, chopped
2 c. asparagus, chopped
1 T. butter
1 T. all-purpose flour
1/2 c. shredded Swiss cheese
1 tomato, chopped

9-inch pie crust, baked
6 eggs
1 c. half-and-half
1/2 t. dried basil
1/2 t. salt
1/8 t. pepper

In a large skillet over medium heat, sauté onion and asparagus in butter until tender, about 5 minutes. Sprinkle with flour; stir in cheese and tomato. Pour into pie crust and set aside. Whisk together remaining ingredients until well blended; pour evenly over top. Bake at 375 degrees for 30 to 35 minutes. Let stand 5 minutes; cut into wedges.

For a pretty table accent, tuck cheery red potted geraniums
into lunch-size paper bags.

Flaky Cheese Danish

Makes 16 servings

2 8-oz. tubes refrigerated
    crescent rolls, divided
8-oz. pkg. cream cheese,
    softened
1-1/4 c. sugar, divided

1 egg, separated
1 t. vanilla extract
1 t. cinnamon
1/2 c. chopped walnuts

Unroll and separate one tube crescent rolls; arrange in an ungreased 13"x9" baking pan. Press seams together and set aside. Blend together cream cheese, one cup sugar, egg yolk and vanilla; spread evenly over crescent rolls. Unroll remaining rolls and arrange over top of cream cheese mixture. Beat egg white until frothy; brush over crescent rolls. Mix together remaining sugar, cinnamon and walnuts; sprinkle on top. Bake at 350 degrees for 30 minutes. Cut into squares; serve warm.

Serving bacon with breakfast? Dip the strips into cold water
before frying to keep the ends from curling up!

Hearty Creamed Eggs & Toast *Makes 8 to 10 servings*

2 10-3/4 oz. cans cream of
   mushroom soup
1-1/4 c. milk

6 eggs, hard-boiled, peeled
   and sliced
8 to 10 slices bread, toasted

Whisk together soup and milk in a large saucepan over medium heat. Fold in eggs. Cook until mixture is warmed but not boiling, stirring frequently. Serve spooned over toast.

Roomy, old-fashioned pop bottle carriers are just right for toting bottles of syrup or jars of jams & jellies to the breakfast table.

Get Up & Go Granola

Makes 10 cups

1/3 c. maple syrup
1/2 c. oil
zest of 2 oranges
4 c. quick-cooking oats,
    uncooked
2 c. mixed nuts, coarsely
    chopped
1 c. sliced almonds

3/4 c. dried apricots, chopped
3/4 c. dried cherries, chopped
1/3 c. honey
2-1/2 t. cinnamon
1/2 t. nutmeg
1/8 t. salt
2 c. sweetened, flaked coconut,
    toasted

Combine syrup, oil and orange zest in a heavy saucepan; bring to a boil. Boil for one minute; remove from heat. Stir in remaining ingredients except coconut; spread on an ungreased baking sheet. Bake at 350 degrees for 10 to 15 minutes. Remove from oven; sprinkle with coconut and let cool. Break into pieces; store in an airtight container.

A fresh breakfast side dish...fruit kabobs! Just slide pineapple chunks, apple slices, grapes, orange wedges and strawberries onto a wooden skewer. They can even be slipped into breakfast smoothies or frosty juices.

Peach Smoothies

Makes 4 servings

2 c. milk
2 c. frozen sliced peaches
1/4 c. frozen orange juice
    concentrate

1 T. sugar
5 to 6 ice cubes
1/4 t. vanilla extract

Combine all ingredients in a blender container. Cover and blend
until smooth.

Give a "Special Delivery" breakfast to someone under
the weather. Fill a basket with homemade jams or pancake mix
and tuck in a loaf of warm bread. Tie a ribbon around
the handle, then visit a special friend!

Frosty Strawberry Squares

Makes 16 servings

1 c. all-purpose flour
1/4 c. brown sugar, packed
1/2 c. chopped walnuts
1/2 c. butter, melted
2 egg whites
2/3 c. sugar

2 T. lemon juice
10-oz. pkg. frozen strawberries,
   thawed
1 c. whipping cream, whipped
Optional: whole strawberries

Mix together flour, brown sugar, walnuts and butter; set aside
one-third for topping. Pat remaining mixture into an ungreased
13"x9" baking pan. Bake at 350 degrees for 20 minutes, stirring
occasionally; remove from oven and set aside. Combine egg whites,
sugar, lemon juice and strawberries in a large bowl. Blend with an
electric mixer on high speed until stiff peaks form, about 10 minutes.
Fold in whipped cream; spoon over crumb crust. Top with reserved
mixture; freeze for 6 hours or overnight. Cut into squares for serving.
If desired, garnish with whole berries.

Egg dishes have a kind of elegance, a freshness, an allure which
sets them quite apart from any other kind of food.
–Elizabeth David

Cheesy Brunch Eggs

Makes 12 servings

1/4 c. half-and-half
1 doz. eggs
pepper to taste

3/4 c. shredded Cheddar cheese
2 T. shredded Parmesan cheese

Spray a 12-cup muffin tin or 12 custard cups with non-stick vegetable spray. Spoon one teaspoon half-and-half into each cup and break an egg into each. With kitchen scissors, cut crosswise through each egg yolk; sprinkle with pepper. Top each egg with one tablespoon Cheddar cheese and one teaspoon Parmesan cheese. Bake at 350 degrees for 15 minutes, until set. Loosen eggs with a rubber spatula and slide onto a warmed serving plate.

A wire basket full of brown eggs makes a terrific
farm-style breakfast centerpiece.

Quick Mini Sausage Wraps   *Makes 8 to 12 servings*

2 16-oz. pkgs. mini smoked   1 lb. bacon, sliced into thirds
   sausages   1/2 c. brown sugar, packed

Wrap each sausage with a piece of bacon; secure with a toothpick.
Arrange on an aluminum foil-lined 13"x9" baking pan; sprinkle
generously with brown sugar. Bake at 350 degrees until bacon is
crisp, about 45 minutes.

Spread some maple butter on fresh pancakes or biscuits.
Just combine 1/2 cup softened butter with 3/4 cup maple syrup
and beat until fluffy...yum!

Down-Home Cornmeal Pancakes *Makes 12 pancakes*

3/4 c. all-purpose flour	3/4 t. salt
1/2 c. cornmeal	5 T. butter
2 T. sugar	1 c. milk
4 t. baking powder	2 eggs

In a large bowl, blend together flour, cornmeal, sugar, baking powder and salt; set aside. In a small saucepan over low heat, melt butter in milk; cool slightly and whisk in eggs. Add wet mixture to dry mixture and blend well. Pour batter by 1/4 cupfuls onto a hot griddle lightly sprayed with non-stick vegetable spray. Cook over medium heat for 2 minutes, until bubbly; flip and cook other side until golden.

Homemade jams & jellies are always welcome hostess gifts!
Wrap the jars with raffia, then glue an old-fashioned fabric yo-yo
on the bow. Top off the yo-yo with a vintage button.

Maple-Blueberry Sauce

Makes 3 cups

1/4 c. brown sugar, packed
1 T. cornstarch
1/2 c. maple syrup
1/2 c. water

2 c. blueberries
1 T. lemon juice
1/8 t. nutmeg

Combine brown sugar and cornstarch in a saucepan; gradually whisk in syrup and water. Cook over medium heat until thick and bubbly; stir in berries, lemon juice and nutmeg. Cook until berries are warmed through; cool slightly.

Cinnamon, Pecan & Honey Syrup

Makes 3 cups

2 c. maple syrup
1/2 c. honey

3/4 c. chopped pecans
1/2 t. cinnamon

Combine all ingredients; mix well.

Enjoy an unhurried breakfast with your family...at dinnertime!
Sit down to scrambled eggs and bacon, a basket of muffins,
fresh fruit and a steamy pot of tea. Perfect!

Mountaintop Bacon

Makes 4 to 6 servings

1/2 c. all-purpose flour
1/4 c. brown sugar, packed

1 t. pepper
1 lb. thick-sliced bacon

Mix flour, brown sugar and pepper together; sprinkle on bacon slices.
Arrange bacon on an aluminum foil-lined baking sheet. Bake at
400 degrees for 10 to 15 minutes, until crisp and golden.

Place violets, lily-of-the-valley and pink miniature roses
in teapots to serve as centerpieces...so sweet.

Homestyle Potato Pancakes

Makes 6 servings

4 c. mashed potatoes
2 eggs, beaten
2 onions, finely chopped

1 t. salt
1/2 t. pepper
1/4 c. olive oil

Combine potatoes, eggs and onions in a medium bowl; stir well to blend. Add salt and pepper. Heat oil in a large skillet over medium heat. Drop potato mixture by 1/4 cupfuls into oil; flatten each to 3/4-inch thick. Cook until golden on both sides.

Use a slow cooker set on low to keep sausage gravy, scrambled eggs or other breakfast foods warm and toasty for brunch.

Sausage Gravy & Biscuits

Makes 4 servings

1 lb. ground pork sausage	salt and pepper to taste
2 T. butter	10-oz. tube refrigerated
1/4 c. all-purpose flour	biscuits, baked
4 c. milk	

Brown sausage in a large skillet over medium heat. Stir in butter until well blended; add flour and stir until mixture is thick. Reduce heat to medium-low and slowly add milk, stirring constantly, until mixture is thick and bubbly. Sprinkle with salt and pepper to taste. Serve over warm, split biscuits.

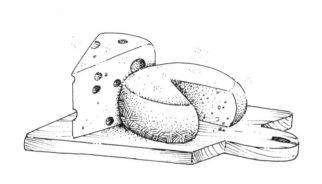

Serve a variety of different cheeses at your brunch...perfect
for guests to nibble on! Line a white-washed basket with red
and white homespun, tie a red ticking bow on the handle and fill
it with an assortment of cheeses and crackers.

Raspberry Coffee Cake

Makes 12 servings

3-oz. pkg. cream cheese
1/4 c. butter
2 c. biscuit mix
1/3 c. plus 1 to 2 T. milk,
    divided

1/2 c. raspberry preserves
1 c. powdered sugar
1/2 t. vanilla extract

Cut cream cheese and butter into biscuit mix until crumbly; blend in 1/3 cup milk. Turn onto a floured surface; knead 8 to 10 times. On wax paper, roll dough out to a 12"x8" rectangle. Turn onto a greased baking sheet; remove wax paper. Spread preserves down center of dough. Make 2-1/2 inch long cuts at one-inch intervals on long sides. Fold strips over preserves. Bake at 425 degrees for 12 to 15 minutes. Stir together powdered sugar, remaining milk and vanilla; drizzle over top. Cut into slices; serve warm.

Nothing helps the scenery like ham and eggs.

-Mark Twain

Cheese & Chive Scrambled Eggs

Makes 4 servings

6 eggs
1 T. dried chives
1/4 t. lemon pepper
1/8 t. garlic salt

1 T. butter
1/3 c. shredded Colby Jack
    cheese
1/3 c. cream cheese, softened

Whisk eggs, chives and seasonings together; set aside. Melt butter in a skillet; add egg mixture. Cook and stir over medium heat until set. Remove from heat; stir in cheeses until melted.

Serve individual-size omelets...pour your ingredients into
lightly greased muffin cups and bake as usual.

Sunny Morn Baked Omelet

Makes 6 to 8 servings

12 slices bread, divided
6 slices deli ham
6 slices American cheese
8 eggs
3 c. milk

1 t. dry mustard
1 t. salt
1/2 c. butter, melted
1 c. corn flake cereal, crushed

Arrange 6 slices bread in the bottom of a greased 13"x9" baking pan; arrange ham and cheese slices on top. Arrange remaining bread slices over cheese; set aside. Combine eggs, milk, mustard and salt; beat well and pour over bread. Cover and refrigerate overnight. Mix together butter and cereal; sprinkle over top. Bake at 350 degrees for 45 minutes.

Cookie cutters make breakfast a treat...use them to
cut out the biscuit dough, shape pancakes or cut shapes from
the centers of French toast. Use mini cutters to make
the sweetest pats of butter!

Amazing Overnight French Toast   *Makes 12 servings*

1 c. corn syrup	6 eggs
1 c. brown sugar, packed	2 c. milk
1 c. butter, sliced	1 t. vanilla extract
12 slices raisin bread	

In a saucepan over medium heat, bring corn syrup, brown sugar and butter to a boil; boil for 5 minutes. Pour into a greased 13"x9" baking pan. Arrange 6 slices bread in pan; top with remaining slices and set aside. Beat eggs, milk and vanilla; pour over bread. Cover and refrigerate overnight. Uncover; bake at 350 degrees for 45 minutes. Serve slices with warm glaze from pan as syrup.

Set the breakfast table the night before....enjoy a relaxed
breakfast in the morning!

Mom's Jam Tea

Makes 4 to 6 servings

4 to 6 t. raspberry jam, divided
1 teapot brewed English
    breakfast tea

sugar to taste
Optional: whipped cream

Place one teaspoon jam in the bottom of each teacup; pour hot tea over jam and stir. Add sugar to taste and top with whipped cream, if desired.

Hosting a Mothers' Day Brunch or a Girls' Tea Party?
Dress up the table by tying pretty scarves around chair backs,
then tuck a tulip in each knot.

Cranberry Scones

Makes 16 scones

2-1/2 c. all-purpose flour	2/3 c. sugar
2-1/2 t. baking powder	3/4 c. buttermilk
1/2 t. baking soda	2/3 c. powdered sugar
3/4 c. butter, sliced	1 T. warm water
1 c. cranberries, chopped	1/4 t. vanilla extract

Mix flour, baking powder and baking soda together in a large bowl; cut in butter until mixture resembles coarse crumbs. Stir in cranberries and sugar; add buttermilk, mixing until just blended. Divide dough in half; on a floured surface, roll each portion into an 8-inch circle, about 1/2-inch thick. Cut each circle into 8 wedges; arrange on ungreased baking sheets. Bake at 400 degrees for 12 to 15 minutes; remove to a wire rack. Combine powdered sugar, warm water and vanilla in a small bowl. Mix to a drizzling consistency, adding a little more warm water if necessary. Drizzle glaze over scones; serve warm.

Slip in a flavored teabag or pressed flowers
with your brunch invitations!

Southwestern Egg Casserole   *Makes 10 to 12 servings*

10 eggs
1/2 c. all-purpose flour
1 t. baking powder
1/8 t. salt
16-oz. pkg. shredded
    Monterey Jack cheese

16-oz. container cottage cheese
1/2 c. butter, melted
2 4-oz. cans chopped green
    chiles, drained
Garnish: sour cream, salsa

Beat eggs in a large bowl and set aside. Combine flour, baking powder and salt in a small bowl; stir into eggs, mixing well. Add cheeses, butter and chiles; pour into a greased 13"x9" baking pan. Bake at 350 degrees until a knife tip inserted in center tests clean, 35 to 40 minutes. Let stand 5 minutes and cut into squares. Garnish as desired with sour cream and salsa.

Floating candles add charm to a breakfast table...float several
in a water-filled yellowware bowl.

Cheesy Chicken Brunch Bake

Makes 6 to 8 servings

10-3/4 oz. can cream of
    chicken soup
3 c. chicken broth
9 slices bread, cubed
4 c. cooked chicken, cubed
1/2 c. instant rice, uncooked

1 c. shredded sharp Cheddar
    cheese, divided
2 T. fresh parsley, minced
1-1/2 t. salt
4 eggs, beaten

Stir together soup and broth in a large bowl. Add bread cubes; toss to coat. Add chicken, rice, 3/4 cup cheese, parsley and salt; mix well. Spread in a greased 13"x9" baking pan. Pour eggs over all; sprinkle with remaining cheese. Bake, uncovered, at 325 degrees for one hour.

For a casual get-together, serve breakfast favorites on
cheery blue and white dishes arranged on homespun placements.
Tuck a bouquet of sunflowers in an old spatterware coffee pot!

Strawberry Popover Pancake

Makes 6 servings

2 T. butter, sliced
1/2 c. all-purpose flour
1/2 c. milk
2 eggs
1/4 c. mini semi-sweet
    chocolate chips

1 pt. strawberries, hulled
    and sliced
1/4 c. sugar
Garnish: frozen whipped
    topping, thawed

Place butter in a 9" glass pie plate and melt in a 200-degree oven; set aside. In a medium bowl, beat flour, milk and eggs until well blended. Pour mixture over melted butter; do not stir. Sprinkle chocolate chips evenly over top. Bake at 400 degrees for 20 to 25 minutes, or until edges are puffed and deep golden. Sprinkle strawberries with sugar and spoon into center of pancake. Cut into wedges; garnish with whipped topping.

Tie silverware together with ribbons in soft colors...peach,
pink, ivory and sage are all pretty!

Banana-Pecan Waffles

Makes 6 waffles

2 eggs
1-1/2 c. buttermilk
1/3 c. butter, melted
1/2 c. banana, mashed
1 t. vanilla extract
2 c. all-purpose flour
2 T. sugar

4 t. baking powder
1/4 t. salt
3/4 c. chopped pecans
Garnish: maple syrup, sliced
    bananas, chopped pecans,
    whipped cream

In a medium bowl, beat eggs for one to 1-1/2 minutes with an electric mixer on medium speed. Blend in remaining ingredients except pecans just until smooth. Pour about 1/2 cup batter onto a preheated waffle iron; sprinkle with pecans and bake as manufacturer directs. Garnish as desired.

"Paint" a face on toast for the kids! Combine one tablespoon
of milk and 3 drops of food coloring, "paint" on bread,
then pop in the toaster!

Make-Ahead Breakfast Eggs

Makes 6 to 8 servings

1 doz. eggs
1/2 c. milk
1/2 t. salt
1/4 t. pepper
1 T. butter

8-oz. container sour cream
12 slices bacon, crisply cooked
  and crumbled
1 c. shredded sharp Cheddar
  cheese

Blend together eggs, milk, salt and pepper; set aside. Melt butter in a skillet over medium-low heat. Add egg mixture and cook until eggs are set but still moist, stirring occasionally. Remove from heat and cool slightly; stir in sour cream. Spoon into a greased 2-quart shallow casserole dish; top with bacon and cheese. Cover and refrigerate overnight. Uncover and bake at 300 degrees for 15 to 20 minutes, until heated through.

Scatter twinkling white lights on your tabletop or across
the mantle for a glittery morning welcome.

Homemade Granola

Makes 8 to 9 cups

2 c. quick-cooking oats,
    uncooked
2 c. whole-grain wheat
    flake cereal
1/4 c. wheat germ
1 c. chopped walnuts

1 c. sunflower kernels
1 c. raisins
1 c. sweetened, flaked coconut
1/4 c. butter
1/2 c. honey
1 t. vanilla extract

Combine first 7 ingredients in an ungreased 13"x9" baking pan; mix well and set aside. Melt together butter, honey and vanilla in a small saucepan over low heat. Pour over mixture in baking pan and toss to coat. Bake at 350 degrees for 20 minutes, stirring after 10 minutes. Let cool; store in an airtight container.

For a pretty brunch table setting, lay a red and white quilt on
your breakfast table. Fill a watering can with wildflowers
and tie a cheery red gingham bow to the handle.
Serve breakfast on old-fashioned spatterware plates.

Frosty Orange Juice

6-oz. container frozen
    orange juice concentrate,
    partially thawed
1 c. milk

1 c. water
1 t. vanilla extract
1/3 c. sugar
12 ice cubes

Combine all ingredients in a blender container. Cover and blend
until frothy.

Hosting a bridal brunch? Scatter confetti and small paper
wedding bells on the buffet table!

Dad's Favorite Roast Beef Hash   *Makes 6 servings*

1/2 c. onion, chopped
2 T. butter
1-1/2 c. potatoes, peeled
    and diced
3 c. roast beef, diced

2 t. Worcestershire sauce
1 t. salt
1/2 t. pepper
1 c. milk or beef broth
1/2 c. beef gravy

In a large skillet over medium heat, cook onion in butter for 3 to 4 minutes. Add potatoes, beef, sauce, salt and pepper to skillet. Stir in milk or broth and gravy; mix well. Bring to a boil over medium heat. Reduce heat and simmer, uncovered, for 20 minutes, or until liquid is absorbed and potatoes are tender.

Wrap glass votives with strands of copper or gold wire.
Easy to find at hardware stores, the wire adds a pretty
sparkle to the breakfast table!

Cinnamon Streusel Coffee Cake   *Makes 15 servings*

3-1/4 c. all-purpose flour,
    divided
2 T. baking powder
1/2 t. salt
1-1/2 c. sugar
3/4 c. butter, divided

2 eggs, beaten
1 c. milk
2 t. vanilla extract
1 c. brown sugar, packed
4 t. cinnamon

Mix 3 cups flour, baking powder, salt and sugar in a large bowl.
Cut in 1/2 cup butter until mixture resembles cornmeal. Blend in
eggs, milk and vanilla; stir just enough to combine thoroughly.
Spread evenly into a greased and floured 13"x9" baking pan. For
topping, mix brown sugar, remaining flour and cinnamon; melt
remaining butter and stir in. Sprinkle topping over batter; bake at
375 degrees for 25 to 30 minutes. Cut into squares; serve warm.

Visit a nearby farmers' market for fresh fruits &
vegetables, baked goods, jams & jellies...perfect for
a farm-fresh breakfast!

Cheesy Scramblin' Pizza

Makes 6 to 8 servings

6 eggs
1/4 c. milk
1/4 c. green onion, sliced
1 tomato, chopped
12-inch Italian pizza crust

8-oz. pkg. pasteurized process
    cheese spread, cubed
6 slices bacon, cut into 1-inch
    pieces and crisply cooked

Whisk together eggs, milk, onion and tomato; pour into a non-stick
skillet sprayed with non-stick vegetable spray. Cook over medium-low
heat until eggs are set, stirring occasionally; set aside. Place pizza
crust on an ungreased baking sheet. Top with egg mixture and cheese;
sprinkle with bacon. Bake at 450 degrees for 10 minutes, or until
cheese is melted. Cut into wedges to serve.

Arrange a generous bunch of zinnias and dwarf sunflowers in
a Mason jar and tie with jute for a cheery tabletop bouquet.

Quick Jam Turnovers

Makes one dozen

12-oz. tube refrigerated biscuits   2 T. milk
3/4 c. strawberry jam   Garnish: sugar

On an ungreased baking sheet, flatten each biscuit with a fork to twice its original size. Place one tablespoon jam in the center of each biscuit; fold biscuits in half and seal edges with a fork. Brush tops with milk; sprinkle with sugar. Bake at 375 degrees for 12 to 15 minutes.

When enjoying brunch or breakfast outside, keep pesky insects away from pitchers of juice. Stitch 4 large beads to the corners of a table napkin and drape over your open pitcher.

Cinnamon-Sugar Doughnuts

Makes 2-1/2 dozen

2 T. oil
8-oz. tube refrigerated biscuits,
    quartered

1/4 c. sugar
1 to 2 t. cinnamon

Heat oil in a skillet over medium-high heat; add quartered biscuits a few at a time. Cook until puffy and golden on both sides. Drain on paper towels; repeat with remaining biscuits. Combine sugar and cinnamon in a small bowl; roll doughnuts to coat. Serve warm.

I have 3 chairs in my house...one for solitude,
2 for friendship, 3 for company.
-Henry David Thoreau

Easy Sticky Buns

Makes 1-1/2 dozen

18 frozen dinner rolls
3-1/2 oz. pkg. cook & serve
    butterscotch pudding mix

1/2 c. butter, melted
1/2 c. brown sugar, packed
1 t. cinnamon

Arrange frozen rolls in a greased Bundt® pan; sprinkle with pudding mix and set aside. Combine butter, brown sugar and cinnamon; pour over rolls. Cover tightly with greased aluminum foil and let rise overnight. Uncover and bake at 350 degrees for 30 to 40 minutes. Carefully invert onto a serving platter. Serve warm.

We all love breakfast foods, so take the time to linger over them! A basket of muffins, fresh fruit and a steamy pot of tea...an ideal way to spend a quiet morning.

Buenos Días Burritos

Makes 4 to 6 servings

3 potatoes, peeled, cooked
   and diced
2 T. oil
1/2 lb. ground mild or hot pork
   sausage, browned and
   drained

4 to 5 eggs
1/2 c. milk
3/4 c. shredded Cheddar cheese
8 to 12 6-inch corn tortillas
Garnish: sour cream, salsa

In a skillet over medium heat, sauté potatoes in oil until golden.
Stir in sausage; heat through. Beat together eggs and milk;
pour into skillet. Reduce heat; cook and stir to desired doneness.
Sprinkle with cheese and cover until cheese is melted. Spread
tortillas with sour cream and salsa; top with egg mixture and
roll up.

Hollowed-out fruits make refreshing individual serving bowls.
Toss together blueberries, sliced strawberries, mandarin
oranges and pineapple tidbits...spoon into scooped-out
grapefruit or orange halves.

Mini Cheddar & Ham Quiches

Makes 2 dozen

2 9-inch refrigerated pie
   crusts, unbaked
2 eggs
1/2 c. milk
3/4 c. zucchini, chopped
1/2 c. mushrooms, chopped

1/2 c. shredded Cheddar cheese
1/4 c. cooked ham, diced
1/4 c. green onion, sliced
1 clove garlic, minced
salt and pepper to taste

Roll out pie crusts into a 12"x12" square on a lightly floured surface.
With a glass tumbler or a biscuit cutter, cut each square into 12 circles.
Press into greased mini muffin cups; set aside. Whisk together eggs
and milk; stir in remaining ingredients. Spoon about one tablespoon
egg mixture into each muffin cup. Bake at 375 degrees for 15 to
18 minutes, until puffed and golden. Cool in cups for 2 to 3 minutes;
remove carefully and serve warm.

A muffin tin makes a sweet centerpiece...simply place a votive candle in each cup. Mix up candle colors for a festive look.

Sugarplum Bacon

Makes 16 pieces

1/2 c. brown sugar, packed   8 slices bacon, halved
1 t. cinnamon

Combine sugar and cinnamon in a small bowl. Dip each piece of
bacon into mixture to coat; twist and place on a broiler pan lined
with aluminum foil. Bake at 350 degrees for 15 to 20 minutes, until
bacon is crisp and sugar is bubbly. Cool on a separate length of
aluminum foil.

Look for distinctive platters, bowls or even a whole set of dishes to use for breakfast or brunch. Years from now, your children and grandchildren will cherish these dishes for the memories they bring back.

Spicy Potato Cakes

Makes 8 to 10 servings

10 potatoes, peeled and grated
1 onion, chopped
2 eggs, beaten
1-1/2 c. all-purpose flour
1/8 t. salt
1/8 t. pepper

1/8 t. dried oregano
1/8 t. dried parsley
1/8 t. garlic powder
1/8 t. garlic salt
1/8 t. onion salt
oil for deep frying

Mix all ingredients except oil together and set aside. Pour oil 1/4-inch deep into a large skillet; heat over medium heat. Drop potato mixture into hot oil by tablespoonfuls. Cook until golden on both sides.

Invite new neighbors to share your next hearty breakfast!
Send them home with a gift basket filled with flyers from
favorite bakeries and pizza parlors, coupons and local maps.

Cheese Blintz Casserole

Makes 6 servings

1-1/4 c. all-purpose flour
1 t. baking powder
3 T. sugar
1/2 c. plus 2 T. butter,
    softened and divided
3/4 c. milk

3 eggs, divided
16-oz. container cottage cheese
1 T. sour cream
1/2 t. salt
Optional: raspberry jam,
    warmed, or fresh berries

Combine flour, baking powder, sugar and 1/2 cup butter in a medium bowl. Mix well; stir in milk and 2 eggs. Set aside. Stir together cottage cheese, sour cream, salt, remaining butter and egg in a separate bowl; set aside. Spoon half the flour mixture into a lightly greased 9"x9" baking pan; top with cottage cheese mixture, then with remaining flour mixture. Bake, uncovered, at 350 degrees for 50 minutes, or until puffy and golden. Let cool slightly; cut into squares. If desired, top with jam or berries.

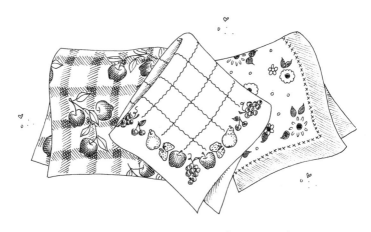

Bring out Mom's printed tablecloths from the 1950's
and use them...they're much too fun to hide away.
Red strawberries, cowboys & cowgirls and other whimsical
designs will delight your family & friends!

Jump-Start Pizza

Makes 8 servings

8-oz. tube refrigerated crescent
   rolls, separated
28-oz. pkg. frozen shredded
   hashbrowns with peppers
   and onions, partially thawed
   and divided
6 slices bacon, crisply cooked
   and crumbled

4-oz. can diced green chiles,
   drained
1/2 to 1 c. shredded Cheddar
   cheese
5 eggs, beaten

Arrange crescent rolls to cover the bottom of an ungreased 12" pizza pan; press seams together and pinch edges to form a slight rim. Spread half the hashbrowns evenly over crust; reserve remainder for another recipe. Sprinkle with bacon, chiles and cheese; carefully pour eggs over top. Bake at 375 degrees for 30 to 35 minutes. Slice into wedges to serve.

Set out whipped cream and shakers of cinnamon and cocoa for coffee drinkers. Tea drinkers will love honey and lemon slices.

Creamy Hot Cocoa

Makes 4 servings

1-1/3 c. semi-sweet chocolate chips	1 t. vanilla extract
4 t. butter	1 qt. half-and-half

Combine chocolate chips, butter and vanilla in the top of a double boiler. Stir over low heat until chocolate is melted and smooth. Gradually add half-and-half; warm through, but do not boil.

For the prettiest arrangement, use Grandma's teacups! Group several teacups together and float a single large blossom in each.

Grandmother's Cinnamon Toast

Makes 4 servings

1/4 c. sugar
1 T. cinnamon

5 T. butter, softened
4 slices bread

Combine sugar and cinnamon in a small bowl. Mix butter with one tablespoon sugar mixture. Spread butter mixture on bread; sprinkle with remaining sugar mixture. Place on a broiler pan and broil for 3 to 4 minutes, until crisp and golden. Makes 4 servings.

Life is like a cup of tea,
it's all in how you make it.
-Irish proverb

Cinnamon-Apple Oatmeal

Makes 4 to 6 servings

1/2 c. applesauce
3/4 c. sugar
2 eggs
3 c. quick-cooking oats,
   uncooked
2 t. baking powder

1/2 t. salt
1/2 t. cinnamon
1 c. milk
1 c. apples, cored, peeled
   and chopped

Combine applesauce, sugar and eggs with an electric mixer on low speed until well blended. Add remaining ingredients except apples and beat well. Fold in apples; pour into a greased 8"x8" baking pan. Bake at 400 degrees for 30 minutes. Serve warm.

Need a centerpiece in a jiffy? Simply arrange slices of orange,
lemon or lime inside a tall clear glass jar, fill with water
and light a floating candle on top.

Chocolate Gravy & Biscuits   *Makes 8 to 10 servings*

3 c. sugar
1/4 c. all-purpose flour
1/4 c. baking cocoa
3 c. milk
1 t. vanilla extract
1 T. butter
10-oz. tube refrigerated
    biscuits, baked

Mix sugar, flour, cocoa and milk in a microwave-safe container.
Microwave on high setting for 8 to 10 minutes, until thick and bubbly;
stir every 2 to 3 minutes. Remove from microwave; stir in vanilla
and butter. To serve, crumble biscuits onto individual serving plates;
spoon gravy over biscuits.

You're Invited!

What: _____

When: _____

Where: _____

RSVP: _____

*Invite family & friends to
a breakfast or brunch get-together with this copy-and-color invitation!*

From the kitchen of: _____

_____

_____

_____

_____

_____

_____

_____

_____

_____

_____

Send your guests home with a recipe
from your time together!

INDEX

INDEX

How Did Gooseberry Patch Get Started?

Gooseberry Patch started in 1984 one day over the backyard fence in Delaware, Ohio. We were next-door neighbors who shared a love of collecting antiques, gardening and country decorating. Though neither of us had any experience (Jo Ann was a first-grade school teacher and Vickie, a flight attendant & legal secretary), we decided to try our hands at the mail-order business. Since we both had young children, this was perfect for us. We could work from our kitchen tables and keep an eye on the kids too! As our children grew, so did our "little" business. We moved into our own building in the country and filled the shelves to the brim with kitchenware, candles, gourmet goodies, enamelware, bowls and our very own line of cookbooks, calendars and organizers. We're so glad you're a part of our **Gooseberry Patch** family!

For a free copy of our **Gooseberry Patch**
catalog, write us, call us or visit us online at:

Gooseberry Patch
600 London Rd.
★ P.O. Box 190 ★
Delaware, OH 43015

1·800·854·6673
www.gooseberrypatch.com